*The Life and Times of*

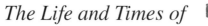
# THOMAS JEFFERSON

## Mitchell Lane
### PUBLISHERS
P.O. Box 196 · Hockessin, Delaware 19707

# Titles in the Series

*The Life and Times of*

*The Life and Times of*

# THOMAS JEFFERSON

## Russell Roberts

*Mitchell Lane*
**PUBLISHERS**

Printing     1     2     3     4     5     6     7     8     9

Library of Congress Cataloging-in-Publication Data
Roberts, Russell, 1953–
    The life and times of Thomas Jefferson / by Russell Roberts.
        p. cm. — (Profiles in American history)
    Includes bibliographical references and index.
    ISBN 1-58415-439-X (library bound)
    1. Jefferson, Thomas, 1743–1826—Juvenile literature. 2. Presidents—United States—Biography—Juvenile literature. I. Title. II. Series.
E332.79.R63 2007
973.4'6092—dc22                                                        2006006110

ISBN-10: 1-58415-439-X                              ISBN-13: 9781584154396

**ABOUT THE AUTHOR: Russell Roberts** has written and published nearly 40 books for adults and children on a variety of subjects, including baseball, memory power, business, New Jersey history, and travel. The lives of American figures of distinction is a particular area of interest for him. He has written numerous books for Mitchell Lane Publishers, including *Nathaniel Hawthorne, George Rogers Clark, Holidays and Celebrations in Colonial America, Daniel Boone,* and *The Lost Continent of Atlantis.* He lives in Bordentown, New Jersey, with his family and a fat, fuzzy, and crafty calico cat named Rusti.

**PHOTO CREDITS:** Cover, pp. 1, 16, 22, 26, 29—Library of Congress; p. 6—West Point Museum Art Collection/United States Military Academy; pp. 15, 36—Barbara Marvis; p. 40—Sharon Beck.

**PUBLISHER'S NOTE:** This story is based on the author's extensive research, which he believes to be accurate. Documentation of such research is contained on page 46.
    The internet sites referenced herein were active as of the publication date. Due to the fleeting nature of some web sites, we cannot guarantee they will all be active when you are reading this book.

PLB

# Profiles in American History

# Contents

*For Your Information

*Thomas Jefferson later in life. Though Jefferson was not fond of public speaking, his writing talents earned him a place in the political spotlight. A pamphlet he wrote,* A Summary View of the Rights of British America, *also earned him a price on his head—for committing treason against King George III of England.*

# CHAPTER 1

## The Enemy Approaches

It was sunrise in early June 1781. The Revolutionary War between Britain and the United States was raging. As part of England's strategy to try to snuff out the American rebellion in the south, British troops had invaded Virginia and forced the state government to scatter from Richmond to Charlottesville. Thomas Jefferson, the governor of Virginia, was near Charlottesville in his stately home, Monticello. With him were Patrick Henry and several other Virginia legislators.

Unexpectedly, in the early daylight, a rider on horseback galloped up to Monticello. His horse was panting heavily as the rider dismounted and scrambled up to the door, a look of extreme anxiety on his face.

The rider was Captain Jack Jouett of the Virginia militia, his young face streaked with angry red cuts and welts from whipping past branches and bushes in his race through the darkened forest to Monticello. He had overheard the dreaded British Green Dragoons' plans to try to capture Jefferson and the legislators. Immediately, Jouett had mounted his horse and risked a gallop through the forest at night to warn them.

The governor did not panic. Quickly he sent his wife and young daughters away from Monticello and arranged the transfer of the state government to the town of Staunton. Then, telescope by his side, he spent the next few hours arranging for the safety of his most

important papers. According to one story, he even sat down and had breakfast.

Periodically Jefferson used the telescope to search the forests and brush of Monticello for any signs that enemy troops were approaching. At the same time two of Jefferson's slaves, Martin and Caesar, were trying to hide as many of Monticello's valuables as possible under the floor of the front portico of the house. Martin stood on the portico above and handed the items down to Caesar. They knew that at any minute, British soldiers could burst from the trees and take everyone in the house as prisoner.

Suddenly Jefferson stiffened. He had been looking through the telescope when he saw the familiar green and red uniforms of the British dragoons begin the climb up the hill to Monticello. The enemy was fast approaching.

Jefferson still did not panic. However, he realized time was running out. He mounted his horse and rode off into the distance, out of danger. Meanwhile, Martin knew that the British troops were close by. He lowered the porch plank back into place before letting Caesar come out. Caesar remained in that dark hole, without food or water, for the next eighteen hours.

Jefferson had done the best he could under difficult circumstances. As he rode away, he had no way of knowing that the episode would come back to haunt him in later years. It would be a major stain upon an otherwise superb record of public service . . . and would almost cost him the United States presidency.

# Poplar Forest

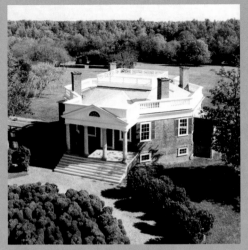

Monticello, the private residence of Thomas Jefferson, is one of the most famous homes in American history. Less well known is Jefferson's other home, which he loved just as much, called Poplar Forest (left).

Monticello, while Jefferson's pride and joy, was often so overrun with visitors both invited and uninvited that Jefferson had difficulty finding the peace and quiet he so desperately craved there. He created a second, much more private residence, at Poplar Forest.

Jefferson's wife, Martha, inherited Poplar Forest, a 4,819-acre plantation near Lynchburg, Virginia, in 1773 following the death of her father. In 1806, when Jefferson was in his second presidential term, he began planning his new home there. In fact, in that year he even took a break from his presidential duties to help masons lay the foundations for the new home.

The residence that Jefferson designed was unique among American homes. It featured five rooms—Jefferson's bedroom, parlor, east bedroom, northeast room, and northwest room—around a central dining room. The home was in the form of an octagon: It had eight sides. Reportedly it was the first eight-sided home in America. It also had another new idea for America: a skylight.

It took many years for Jefferson to complete Poplar Forest. There he led the type of life he had always wanted to lead. In the morning he rode his horse, read, or wrote letters. He ate around three or four o'clock in the afternoon, and then spent the rest of the day wandering about the plantation and perhaps writing more letters or reading until he went to bed around ten o'clock in the evening.

With the exception of family members, almost no other visitors were allowed at Poplar Forest. Most people did not even know it existed. It was Jefferson's private place. His neighbors knew that he craved privacy, and they never bothered him. Sometimes they would join him for dinner, bringing cider, cheese, or fruit.

In 1823, Jefferson's grandson Francis Eppes and his wife, Elizabeth, began living at Poplar Forest. Jefferson himself visited the plantation for the final time that year.

For Your Information

*Several American presidents attended the College of William and Mary, including Thomas Jefferson, James Monroe, and John Tyler. Another president, George Washington, was the chancellor of the college for eleven years.*

# CHAPTER
## 2

## Gentleman Farmer

Thomas Jefferson was born in April 1743 at Shadwell, five miles east of Charlottesville, in Goochland County, Virginia. The county later changed its name to Albemarle. Initially the date of his birth was April 2. However, that day changed in 1758 when England adopted the new Gregorian calendar, which moved all dates forward 11 days. The date of Jefferson's birth became April 13.

Thomas' mother was Jane Randolph Jefferson. Historians know little about her, and Jefferson rarely mentioned her. He reported her death in 1776 in one line in a letter.

On the other hand, he enjoyed telling stories about his father, Peter Jefferson, a mapmaker and surveyor. Peter was a man of great strength, who passed on to Thomas the gift of good health. All his life Thomas Jefferson was an extremely healthy man who believed that a person maintained his health through walking and two hours of brisk exercise per day. He also believed in eating mainly fruits and vegetables, using meat more as a seasoning than as a main course.

Thomas was the oldest son. He had two older sisters, three younger brothers, and four younger sisters, but two of his brothers died in infancy. As a child, Thomas enjoyed riding horses, canoeing, and especially music. By age nine he could already play the violin. He often played violin while his sister Jane sang. He never lost his

love of the instrument. For years he practiced the violin several hours per day.

As he got older, he grew into a tall, lean, young man with red hair and hazel eyes. On August 14, 1757, when Thomas was fourteen, his father died at the age of forty-nine or fifty. Peter had always stressed the importance of education, and his death did not stop Thomas's schooling. A tutor taught young Jefferson Greek, Latin, math, literature, and other subjects.

In 1760 Jefferson went to the College of William and Mary in Williamsburg, Virginia. While there, he met another student and violin player named Patrick Henry. The two entertained other students with their violin playing. At college, Jefferson developed his lifelong love of books. He would read for an hour in the morning before breakfast.

Also at William and Mary, Jefferson met a lawyer named George Wythe. He decided to train with Wythe to become a lawyer himself. Wythe became a role model for him. He taught Jefferson not only the law, but also such subjects as history, philosophy, and ethics. After almost five years with him, Jefferson became a lawyer in 1767. For seven years he practiced law, winning many of his cases, but he never really saw himself as a lawyer. Rather, he considered himself a gentleman planter, or farmer. At that time, a gentleman farmer was someone of great intellect and good breeding who either used hired help or slaves to run a farm for him. Meanwhile, as a member of Virginia's upper class, Jefferson had been elected to the House of Burgesses (the legislative body that governed colonial Virginia) in 1769, when he was just twenty-five years old. By the end of 1774, he had retired from practicing law.

Jefferson had been living at his family's home in Shadwell, but in 1768 he began planning his own home. Upon his father's death he had inherited 1,900 acres of land. Choosing a small hill four miles from Shadwell, he began building a home he called Monticello. (*Monticello*, pronounced mon-tih-CHEH-loh, means "little mountain" in Italian.) These efforts accelerated in 1770 when Shadwell burned down. In November that year, Jefferson moved into a tiny living area at Monticello. It was his parlor, kitchen, bedroom, and study.

On January 1, 1772, Jefferson, a highly eligible bachelor, married a twenty-three-year-old wealthy widow named Martha Wayles

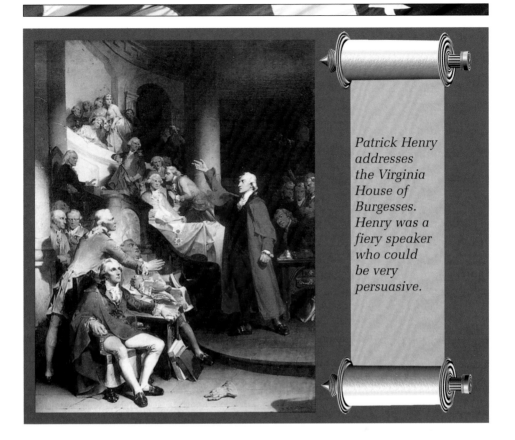

*Patrick Henry addresses the Virginia House of Burgesses. Henry was a fiery speaker who could be very persuasive.*

Skelton. She had large hazel eyes and auburn hair. Sometimes she played musical duets with Jefferson, he on the violin and she on the harpsichord. According to one story, two other men who wanted to marry Martha arrived together at her house. They were on their way to see her when they heard her and Jefferson playing a duet. After listening for a moment, they knew that the two were perfect together, and left the house.

Two weeks after their wedding, the couple arrived at Monticello, which was under construction. Only one room could be lived in. Even so, the couple was happy. Jefferson called her "the cherished companion of my life."[1]

Throughout his life Jefferson kept records about everything, particularly what was happening at Monticello. He kept a "garden book," in which he recorded observations about weather conditions, plantings, and chores to be done.

It was hard making money as a farmer, and even as a gentleman farmer. While the gentleman farmer did not pay his slaves, he was responsible for their food, clothing, and shelter. When money was short, gentlemen farmers often bought on credit. Gradually, these debts accumulated, and the farmers would find themselves owing a great deal of money. Debt would hound Jefferson much of his life.

Jefferson's debt increased in 1773, when his father-in-law, John Wayles, died and Jefferson inherited his lands—lands on which Wayles already owed money. To pay this debt, Jefferson was forced to sell so much land that his estate was cut to half its former size.

Jefferson also inherited Wayles' slaves. One of them was Betty Hemings. Wayles had had a relationship with Betty, and she bore him at least one daughter, named Sally. Sally, who was therefore Martha's half sister, would become a key figure in Jefferson's life.

When Jefferson became a member of the House of Burgesses, he sided with those who did not favor Virginia's royal governor, who represented British rule of the colony. Other members of this group included George Washington and Patrick Henry.

At the time, the British and the colony of Massachusetts were at odds. Riots between the two sides broke out in Boston. Most Americans felt that what happened in Boston did not concern them, but Jefferson had a different view. He realized that all the colonists were Americans, be they from Massachusetts, New Jersey, or Virginia.

The Boston Tea Party, staged in December 1773, soon brought matters between the British and the rebellious Massachusetts Colony to a head. As Britain tried to punish Massachusetts through passage of the so-called Intolerable Acts, people in other colonies realized that what was happening there could happen to them. Virginia, and Jefferson, took the lead in organizing resistance to England. Jefferson helped to draft a resolution calling for a day of fasting and prayer in support of Massachusetts. In response, Lord Dunmore, Virginia's royal governor, dissolved the General Assembly. The members then walked down the street and met in a tavern, where they passed a resolution calling for a continental congress to meet in Philadelphia, America's largest city.

To help guide Virginia's delegates to the congress, Jefferson wrote *A Summary View of the Rights of British America*. His friends thought it summed up the dispute between England and America

*Monticello, Jefferson's house, is one of the most famous homes in America. Jefferson constantly worked on and changed Monticello as ideas and inspirations occurred to him, but the continual work was a drain on his finances.*

so powerfully that they published it as a pamphlet. In it Jefferson argued that the colonists should receive the same rights as British citizens. It challenged King George III to treat Americans fairly. The pamphlet was reprinted in London. When the king's ministers read it, they decided Jefferson was an enemy.

On April 19, 1775, colonial and British forces exchanged gunfire in Lexington and Concord, Massachusetts, starting the Revolutionary War. As relations deteriorated between America and England, Jefferson mainly stayed busy at Monticello. He added on to the house, improved the grounds, and expanded his garden plantings. His household now numbered 117 persons—34 free and 83 slaves.

In the spring of 1776, colonial forces under George Washington prepared to fight British troops. English rule of the colonies had collapsed, and the Continental Congress was getting ready to declare America a free and independent nation. On June 11, 1776, Congress

*These five men composed the committee that was assigned to write a declaration of independence for America. (Left to right) Thomas Jefferson, John Adams, Benjamin Franklin, Robert Livingston, and Roger Sherman.*

named John Adams, Benjamin Franklin, Roger Sherman, Robert Livingston, and Jefferson to a committee to write a declaration of independence.

Jefferson did not have a powerful voice and hated public speaking. Yet because of his literary skill he was chosen to write what would become the loudest cry in history from one people to another. As John Adams noted: "During the whole time I sat with him [Jefferson] in Congress, I never heard him utter three sentences together. It will naturally be inquired how it happened that he was appointed on a committee of such importance. . . . Mr. Jefferson had the reputation of a masterly pen."[2]

The document that this master of the pen produced would become one of the most famous in history.

# Patrick Henry

Jefferson's friend and fellow delegate Patrick Henry (left) has become immortalized because of seven words: "Give me liberty or give me death."

Henry was born on May 29, 1736, in Hanover County, Virginia. He was a self-educated man who at first tried to be a storekeeper and then a farmer. Neither of these professions suited him. He then decided to study law, and in 1760 was admitted to the Virginia bar as a lawyer.

From this point on Henry's rise was meteoric. He was elected to the Virginia House of Burgesses (the colonial legislature), and quickly joined with the so-called rebels that were advocating that America break free of England. He became known as a fiery orator. In 1774, when the House of Burgesses was dissolved, Henry became a member of the revolutionary legislature of Virginia. The following year, he made his speech before the legislature that included the sentence: "I know not what course others may take, but as for me, give me liberty or give me death!"

Ironically, there is speculation that Henry did not utter these famous words. The first time the speech was written was in 1817, more than forty years later, in a biography of Henry by William Wirt called *Life and Character of Patrick Henry*. Reportedly, Wirt wrote the book from the recollections of people, including apparently those who might have been present at that famous speech. However, some historians feel that Wirt basically wrote the speech himself for inclusion in the book.

During the following years Henry was a key figure in the revolutionary struggle. He served five terms as governor of Virginia, was a delegate to the First and Second Continental Congresses, and helped write the new Virginia Constitution. He was also a delegate to the Constitutional Convention, but did not like the final version because he felt it gave too much power to the federal government. Because of this, he played a key role in the adoption of the Bill of Rights to the Constitution. He became a supporter of the Federalist political party, although most of his friends became supporters of anti-federalist Thomas Jefferson.

He was elected to the Virginia House of Delegates in 1799, but died on June 6, 1799, before he could take office.

For Your Information

*An illustration of Martha, Jefferson's wife, to whom he was deeply devoted. Her death at a young age greatly affected Jefferson. He never remarried.*

# CHAPTER 3

## Revolution at Home and Abroad

It took Jefferson seventeen days to write the Declaration of Independence. He worked in the second-floor parlor of a three-story house on Market Street in Philadelphia, which he had rented from bricklayer Jacob Graff (or Graaf). He wrote on a small desk he had designed himself, and which had been built by his African-American carpenter. But there was nothing small about the words he produced. They came to define not just a country and its people, but a way of life for all humanity.

As Jefferson himself said about the Declaration, it was not his intent to say something new or startling. Rather, he wanted "to place before mankind the common sense of the subject, in terms so plain and firm as to command their assent, and to justify ourselves in the independent stand we are compelled to take."[1] The Declaration was, as he said, "to be an expression of the American mind."[2]

To write it, Jefferson combined hard-edged legal and constitutional arguments against the offenses of King George with theories about the natural rights of people. The result was a document that was specific in its list of grievances as well as lofty in its expression of the rights of every human being.

The Declaration of Independence is such a model document, in part, because of the language it uses to lay out the colonies' case against King George. Although the principles on which the document

is based involve complicated ideas of history, law, and philosophy, Jefferson was able to takes these ideas and concepts and write them in language that the common citizen could understand. That, perhaps, is the biggest reason why the Declaration of Independence was so powerful then, and remains such a powerful document today. It speaks to the people in simple, direct, yet extremely persuasive language. An audience hearing it today can feel exactly what colonists felt hundreds of years ago. It is a document for the ages.

Jefferson showed his initial draft declaration to his fellow committee members. John Adams and Benjamin Franklin made suggestions and comments. Jefferson then presented this revised draft to the Congress on June 28, 1776.

Congress made more changes to the document before approving it. Jefferson, proud of his work, treated each change as a personal insult. Franklin tried to cheer up his colleague, but Jefferson silently continued to squirm. Fortunately, Adams, a fiery public speaker, repeatedly defended Jefferson's work before the Congress, perhaps sparing it from even further changes.

July 4, 1776, was a hot day in Philadelphia. The heat only added to the delegates' tension and excitement over the passage of this monumental document. Adding to their discomfort that day were swarms of biting flies from a nearby stable. Jefferson always believed that the delegates signed the Declaration of Independence because they were eager to get out of the room and away from the flies.

On September 2, 1776, Jefferson resigned his seat in Congress. The next day he left for Virginia. He wanted to remain close to home to watch over his wife, who was often in ill health. In Virginia he was elected to the House of Delegates, the lower house of the legislature. He worked on numerous issues, including reforming Virginia's existing laws, defending religious freedom, and establishing a system of public education—the first in America.

On June 1, 1779, the Virginia legislature elected Jefferson governor. His tenure as Virginia's chief executive, however, was perhaps his lowest point in politics. The major reason was the ongoing war with England. Virginia was America's biggest state—its territory included all of present-day Virginia, West Virginia, and Kentucky, plus large parts of Ohio, Indiana, and Illinois. Congress and Washington's army continually asked Jefferson for Virginia men, money, and supplies.

However, Virginians were being threatened by the British in the east and by attacks from Native Americans and others from the west. There was little left for Jefferson to send to Washington's beleaguered army.

In June 1780, Jefferson was reelected governor, but his second term brought him more trouble than the first. The British had shifted their strategy in the war; now they were attacking America in the south instead of the north. In December that year, a British force under American traitor Benedict Arnold invaded Virginia and headed for Richmond. Alarm swept through Virginia as Arnold rampaged throughout the state, forcing Jefferson and the government to flee the city. Arnold did capture Richmond, but he held it only a few days.

In late May 1781, events repeated themselves. The new British commander in Virginia, Lord Cornwallis, sent his Green Dragoons heading toward Monticello to capture Jefferson. Narrowly warned in time, Jefferson and his family just managed to escape. The government fled to the town of Staunton.

At this point Jefferson made an error in judgment. His term as governor had expired, and his successor was not due to be chosen for ten days. He saw himself as a private citizen again, and went home to his wife instead of going to Staunton to turn over power. Thus he left Virginia without a governor until a new governor was elected by the Virginia Assembly some days later.

His actions stunned many Virginians. He was accused of being a coward and running home to be with his wife. Jefferson, his pride wounded, gave a speech on December 12 in which he answered the charges point by point and cleared his name.

The affair made Jefferson swear that he was through with public life forever. In a May 1782 letter to friend James Monroe, he said that the whole thing "had inflicted a wound on my spirit which only will be cured by the all-healing grave."[3]

If things had stayed the same in Jefferson's life, perhaps he would never have returned to public life. Congress kept offering him assignments, but he continually declined. Then one event changed everything.

In August 1782, Martha gave birth to the couple's sixth child, Lucy. Childbirth was difficult in those days, and with this one Martha's shaky health steadily deteriorated. As she worsened, it became clear that she was dying. Martha made Jefferson promise that

*Jefferson goes over the Declaration of Independence with Benjamin Franklin and John Adams. Franklin was an excellent writer, but he let Jefferson write this most important document. The final result showed the wisdom of Franklin's decision.*

he would never remarry, so that her children would not be brought up by a stepmother as she had been. On September 6, 1782, Martha Jefferson died, leaving Thomas with three small daughters: Martha, Mary, and Lucy (three had previously died).

Jefferson suffered an emotional collapse during his wife's illness. For weeks after her death he was delirious. After he recovered, he spent hours roaming the grounds of Monticello, with only nine-year-old Martha as company.

Late in 1782, Congress assigned him as part of an American delegation to Paris to negotiate a peace treaty with England. If his wife had been alive, Jefferson probably would have refused the appointment, but the opportunity to once again get involved in his country's affairs would help ease his grief. Before he could leave for France, however, Franklin, Adams, and John Jay finalized the treaty, officially ending the war.

In June 1783, Jefferson went to Philadelphia as head of the Virginia delegation to the Confederation Congress. (The Confederation Congress was the legislative body that met under the Articles of Confederation.) In Congress he took particular interest in the sparsely inhabited western territories won from Great Britain. He felt that America's future lay in its ability to expand westward. He pushed a plan that allowed those territories to govern themselves until they reached a certain population level. Once they did, they could become states. The idea was adopted, both by the Confederation Congress and a few years later by the Constitutional Convention.

Jefferson had also wanted to ban slavery in the territories and future new states, but the measure was narrowly defeated. He would wrestle with the slavery issue all his life, never quite able to reconcile how a country based on liberty, and a person so committed to personal freedom as he, could keep a race in chains. He worried that divine judgment was forthcoming for the country because of its use of slaves. He wrote: "Indeed I tremble for my country when I reflect that God is just; [and] that his justice cannot sleep for ever."[4]

As much as he may have believed in freedom for the slaves, he also thought that the two races—black and white—could not peacefully coexist. "Nothing is more certainly written in the book of fate than that these people are to be free," he wrote. "Nor is it less certain that the two races, equally free, cannot live in the same government."[5]

On May 7, 1784, Congress named Jefferson to join John Adams and Benjamin Franklin in Paris to negotiate commercial treaties with European nations. With his eldest daughter, Martha, Jefferson traveled to Paris that July.

At first Jefferson was uncomfortable in France. Just as he began to feel at ease, in January 1785 he received word that his youngest daughter, Lucy, had died. Whooping cough had claimed her at age two the previous October.

Again filled with grief, Jefferson threw himself into his work to lessen his pain. Fortunately, both Adams and Franklin liked him, and he them. Adams' wife, Abigail, grew very fond of Jefferson and his daughter, and helped to make them feel at home.

In May, Jefferson was named to succeed Franklin as the American Minister to France. When told that he was replacing the beloved Franklin, Jefferson said: "I succeed; no one can replace him."[6]

Shortly thereafter Adams left France for London to become the new ambassador to Great Britain. When Franklin sailed for home, it left Jefferson, who could barely speak French, all by himself in Paris. "I shall really regret to leave Mr. Jefferson," said Abigail Adams. "He is one of the choice ones of the earth."[7]

Jefferson turned out to be a successful diplomat. He skillfully renegotiated the terms of loans America had taken from other countries to finance the revolution. He reported to Americans what was going on in European countries, and he promoted the United States to skeptics unwilling to believe that a democracy could survive.

Jefferson was a fierce defender of anything American. When Georges-Louis Leclerc, comte de Buffon, a renowned French naturalist, declared that all plant and animal life (including human) was smaller and weaker in America than in Europe, Jefferson sprang to his country's defense. He wrote the only book of his life, entitled *Notes on the State of Virginia*. The book destroyed the claims that plant and animal life was superior in the Old World.

While Jefferson was in Paris, he had his first serious romantic encounter since his wife's death. Maria Cosway, a blue-eyed, curly haired blonde, and Jefferson toured Paris together, visiting art galleries, museums, and theaters. Maria was married, and as a Roman Catholic did not believe in divorce, so although she and Jefferson flirted greatly, that is probably as far as their relationship went.

Jefferson followed news of the 1787 Constitutional Convention in America both anxiously and enviously. He enjoyed creating governments and writing constitutions, and knew that he was missing out on important events in his homeland.

In Paris, Jefferson also saw the opening months of the French Revolution. He had long been appalled by the gap in France between rich and poor. He considered revolution as a way for the common people to keep government in line. He was delighted that France was trying to experiment with liberty and democracy, just as America had done. He hoped that France would become a beacon of democracy that would inspire other European countries to follow suit.

As 1789 drew to a close, Jefferson prepared to return home to the United States. He intended to return to France as minister, but waiting for him in America was a much different political climate than the one he had left.

# Jefferson, Slavery, and Sally Hemings

The issue of slavery greatly concerned Thomas Jefferson. On the one hand, he hated slavery and all it stood for. He had criticized slavery in the Declaration of Independence, and was in favor of banning the importation of more slaves. Yet he used slaves and slave labor at Monticello.

Nowhere was Jefferson's conflicting feelings on slavery more on display than in one of the greatest historical controversies of all time. Was he the father of some or all of his slave Sally Hemings' children? The question has been raging for over 200 years. Recent DNA tests have done nothing to quiet the controversy.

The charge that Jefferson had fathered children with one of his slaves first became public in 1802. James Callendar, the editor of a Virginia newspaper, printed the charge in an attempt to discredit Jefferson. But Callendar had a reputation as a man who would print anything, so it was easy to dismiss the charge. Jefferson admirers and supporters claimed it was simply a vicious rumor.

Then in 1974, a long-ignored 1873 interview by Madison Hemings (Sally's son and a slave freed in Jefferson's will), in which he claimed that Jefferson was the father of Sally's children, was reprinted in Fawn Brodie's biography about Jefferson. This reignited the controversy to a fever pitch.

Several years later, modern science entered the picture. An article in the November 1998 British science journal *Nature* published the results of a DNA study that seemed to prove, along with other evidence, that Jefferson was the father of at least one of Sally's children. The Thomas Jefferson Memorial Foundation concluded that there was a strong possibility that Jefferson was the father of at least one and perhaps all of the children of Sally Hemings (left).

Others pointed out that the study did not prove that Thomas Jefferson fathered the children—only that a Jefferson did. Suspicion has fallen on Thomas's brother Randolph; his first cousin once removed George; and others with the same DNA. Because of the continuing questions, in May 2002 the Monticello Association (descendants of Thomas Jefferson) voted not to admit Sally Hemings' descendants into their organization. This is where the controversy currently stands.

Alexander Hamilton was Jefferson's great rival during the presidency of George Washington. Hamilton, as Secretary of the Treasury, and Jefferson, as Secretary of State, clashed on many issues.

# CHAPTER
# 4

## Hamilton and Home

Jefferson arrived back in America, at Norfolk, Virginia, on November 23, 1789. Waiting for him was a letter from the new president, George Washington, informing him that he had been chosen as Secretary of State in Washington's cabinet. Although he had wanted to return to France, he reluctantly put those plans aside.

Before leaving Monticello for the nation's temporary capital city of New York, he presided over the wedding of seventeen-year-old Martha to Thomas Mann Randolph. He did not arrive in New York until March 21, 1790.

Governing under the Constitution was new, and Jefferson and the other cabinet secretaries had much to set up and establish so that America could operate properly. As secretary of state, he would be responsible for establishing national systems of coinage, weights, and measures. Jefferson proposed the system of decimal coinage (one hundred cents = one dollar) that is still in use today. However, his plan for establishing weights and measures based on the metric system was turned down.

Jefferson often found himself working with the other cabinet secretaries, including Attorney General Edmund Randolph and Secretary of War Henry Knox. However, he most often had to deal with the youthful Secretary of the Treasury—Alexander Hamilton.

Hamilton was everything Jefferson was not. Intense whereas Jefferson was reserved, Hamilton was not a Virginia planter like so many Revolutionary heroes but a native of the West Indies. He had spent four years during the Revolution as Washington's chief aide. After that he became a lawyer and one of the leading voices calling for ratification of the new Constitution.

At first Jefferson and Hamilton worked well together. Both knew that the biggest problem facing the new nation was the large debt it had accumulated during the war. Hamilton came up with a plan that paid off the debt, but it faced tough going in Congress. In exchange for Jefferson's support of his debt plan, Hamilton agreed to let the site of the new capital city be on the Potomac River between Maryland and Virginia, instead of farther north. Once the site was fixed, Jefferson worked with Frenchman Major Pierre Charles L'Enfant on the design of the city that eventually became Washington, D.C.

After that agreement, the relationship between Hamilton and Jefferson deteriorated. In the summer of 1790, Spain seized four British ships in Canada, claiming they had crossed into Spanish territory. Both Spain and Great Britain appealed to the United States to help them avoid war over the incident. Jefferson hoped to use the affair to win concessions from both countries on trade and other matters, but Hamilton spoiled his plans. He told the British ambassador that he would step in should Jefferson prove too harsh with England.

The first serious break between them occurred in the winter of 1791. Washington was uncertain whether or not to sign a bill creating a Bank of the United States, because the Constitution did not specifically call for one. He asked both Jefferson and Hamilton for their opinions. Jefferson held to a strict view of the Constitution and argued that the bill should be vetoed. Hamilton, however, maintained that the Constitution gave Congress the power to do what is "necessary and proper," and that the bank fell under those guidelines. Thus convinced, Washington signed the bill.

Jefferson and Hamilton were passionate about their views of the United States, its people, and its government. Jefferson felt that the people were the source of the government's dedication to freedom and liberty; he wanted America to remain a nation of small farmers, with the states and not a distant federal government having most of

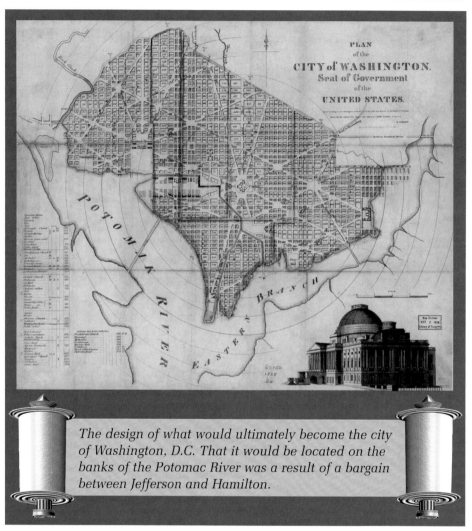

*The design of what would ultimately become the city of Washington, D.C. That it would be located on the banks of the Potomac River was a result of a bargain between Jefferson and Hamilton.*

the power. Hamilton, however, felt that only a strong central government based on industrial might could help the United States become a world power.

Another division between the two came over whether or not the U.S. should support the French Revolution. Jefferson felt that the French Revolution was a true people's uprising that had the same basis in freedom and democracy as the American Revolution, so the U.S. should support it. Hamilton wanted the U.S. to stay neutral.

As Jefferson and Hamilton battled, so did their supporters throughout the government. Those who aligned with Jefferson called

themselves Republicans, feeling that they were the true representatives of republican government. Hamilton and his defenders became known as Federalists. The roots of political parties were thus planted in American politics as the two sides drifted further apart.

Jefferson noted that he and Hamilton were "pitted against each other like two fighting cocks."[1] Washington was caught in the middle of their increasingly vicious battles. In August 1792, he wrote to both Jefferson and Hamilton, asking them to stop arguing. The responses of both indicated how passionately each felt that he was in the right. Hamilton said: "I consider myself as the deeply injured party . . . I have been an object of uniform opposition from Mr. Jefferson, from the first moment of his coming to the City of New York. . . ."[2]

Jefferson sounded a similarly angry note: "I will not suffer my retirement to be clouded by the slanders of a man whose history, from the moment at which history can stoop to notice him, is a tissue of machinations [lies] . . ."[3]

Washington realized there would be no letup in the bickering. "I have a great, a sincere esteem for you both,"[4] he replied.

Both Jefferson and Hamilton felt that the other was trying to drive him from the government. Jefferson grew tired of the continual confrontation. He wanted to step down from his position as secretary of state, but kept postponing it because he did not want it to seem as if Hamilton had forced him to leave. At the end of July, 1793, he offered his resignation to Washington, but the president managed to persuade him to stay on until the end of the year.

Those last months were filled with controversy because of the French Revolution. French revolutionaries had executed the former king and queen of France in January 1793. Hamilton argued that since the United States had had a treaty with the old French government, the execution of the king as the leader of that government canceled the treaty. Jefferson disagreed, saying that the treaty was with the French nation, not its king. Washington agreed with Jefferson; but he still issued a proclamation that America would remain neutral even as other nations were declaring war on France.

The Genet affair nearly changed his mind. Edmond Genet was the new French minister to the United States. He toured the country raising money to build French ships to attack those of other countries, and seeking sailors to crew the ships. Some Americans favored

France, while others did not. It was a matter of great political debate, and Genet's conduct threatened to overheat the already smoldering attitudes in the United States toward the French Revolution.

At first Jefferson tried to defend Genet, but he soon realized the argument would destroy whatever tolerance Washington had for France and its increasingly violent revolution. He backed a decision demanding that France recall Genet.

Jefferson urged others to take on Hamilton also. He implored his ally James Madison to "take up your pen . . . and cut him to pieces."[5]

The Genet affair was the final straw for Jefferson. Weary of the backbiting and bickering, he resigned as Secretary of State. On January 5, 1794, he left for Monticello, claiming he would never again serve in public life. As he wrote in September, 1794: "No circumstance . . . will ever more tempt me to engage in anything public."[6]

When he returned home, Jefferson discovered that both the house and grounds were in shabby shape. He blamed the condition on his long absence and set about repairing them. One improvement was replacing the high-maintenance rail fences that marked his property line with rows of trees. Over the next three years he planted more than a thousand peach trees, plus numerous other trees such as apple and cherry. Not only did the trees look nicer, but they provided him with plenty of fresh fruit.

Now that he had the time, Jefferson was also able to indulge his talent for invention. He designed a new type of plow that cut through the soil easier. He tried developing a mechanical threshing machine to better separate the grain from the chaff of harvested wheat.

At Monticello, free from the demands of public life, Jefferson surrounded himself with the things he loved: friends like James Madison and James Monroe, his farm, and his family. Martha gave him a grandchild, Thomas Jefferson Randolph. Her second child, baby daughter Ellen Wayles Randolf, died in July 1795.

Inspired by Europe's impressive architecture during his time in France, Jefferson decided to rebuild Monticello. The project would consume most of the rest of his life and become a serious financial drain. The house he designed was a domed, two-story building that looked from the outside as if it were just one story. His slaves did all the physical labor, from demolishing the old house, making bricks for the new one, putting up the walls, building new furniture, and performing the carpentry.

Interestingly, while Jefferson relied on slaves for rebuilding and operating Monticello, he also apparently tried to pretend as if slavery did not exist there. The estate's landscaping and covered walkways concealed the slave quarters from the view of the main house. He also installed several devices in the house, such as a dining room dumbwaiter, so that he would not have to see slaves.

Although Jefferson continued to insist that he was happy as a private citizen at Monticello, little by little he inched toward a return to public life. When Washington and Hamilton led troops into Pennsylvania to crush the Whiskey Rebellion, Jefferson was horrified by what he considered an abuse of the central government's power. He hailed efforts to defeat a treaty with England that he thought was too pro-British.

Washington announced that he was retiring in 1796. The two obvious choices for the presidency were Jefferson as the leader of the Republicans and Vice President John Adams as head of the Federalists. Presidential elections were decided solely by electors, who were chosen by the legislatures of each state. There was not a popular vote.

In the election, Adams received 71 electoral votes to Jefferson's 68, while two other candidates, Thomas Pinckney and Aaron Burr, got 59 and 30 votes, respectively. Under the rules, Adams became president while the person with the second-most electoral votes—Jefferson—became vice president. Even though the two had very different political philosophies, they were expected to work together for the good of the country.

Jefferson did not mind taking second place. Being the vice president instead of president would enable him to spend more time at Monticello and to pursue other interests. He became president of the American Philosophical Society, a Philadelphia-based organization founded by Benjamin Franklin that was dedicated to the pursuit of science and research, subjects dear to Jefferson's heart.

As a student of parliamentary law (the rules governing public meetings), Jefferson was the ideal person to preside over meetings of the Senate as vice president. He wrote a booklet, entitled *A Manual*

*Thomas Pickney (left) and Aaron Burr, along with John Adams and Thomas Jefferson, were candidates for U.S. President in the election of 1796. Adams won, and Jefferson came in second.*

*of Parliamentary Practice*, that is still used by the U.S. House of Representatives.

But Jefferson could not escape the world of politics. One of the most serious and damaging to his reputation occurred during what came to be known as the XYZ Affair. France had replaced its revolutionary government with a more conservative one. President Adams, hoping he could finally settle some of America's disputes with France, sent three commissioners there. Once in France, the commissioners met repeated delays until three French diplomats—called X, Y, and Z in an official report—suggested that things could go more smoothly if the Americans paid bribe money. The Americans were outraged. The Federalists used the affair to anger

U.S. citizens against the French and to embarrass Jefferson and the pro-French Republicans.

Another controversy arose over the Alien and Sedition Acts. These laws gave the federal government powers to deport anyone who was not a citizen. They were aimed at all the immigrants streaming into America whom the Federalists feared for their supposedly "dangerous" ideas. The acts also stifled criticism of the government. Jefferson and the Republicans viewed the Alien and Sedition Acts as an assault on liberty, taking the view that any worthwhile government could withstand criticism.

As the election of 1800 approached, it was obvious that Jefferson and Adams were again going to be the two main candidates. The Federalists were hurt by a split between Adams and Hamilton. In October, Hamilton published a pamphlet that called on Federalists to abandon Adams for his running mate, Charles Pinckney.

The result was that the Republican candidates, again Jefferson and Aaron Burr, were the two top vote-getters. They tied, with 73 electoral votes each. The House of Representatives, with its Federalist majority, would have to select one of them for president.

Initially, Republicans expected Burr to step aside and leave the way open for Jefferson. Burr refused to defer. The House repeatedly voted, but each tally came up just short of a majority for Jefferson.

Jefferson was angered by what he felt was Burr's treachery. Meanwhile, rumors circulated that Burr and the Federalists were hatching a deal that would put him into the White House in exchange for Federalist influence in the new government.

Meanwhile, Hamilton was faced with the prospect that one of the two men he hated most in politics would become president. He disliked Burr more, so he urged Federalists not to vote for him.

Finally, a group of Federalist House members devised a plan to break the tie. They cast blank ballots, thus abstaining from the election and letting a majority of the House delegates that participated vote for Jefferson. On February 20, 1801, Jefferson was officially notified that he was the third president of the United States.

# The Federalist Party

The Federalist political party was once the dominant party in America. Today, however, it is nothing more than a memory.

*John Jay*

The party was started in the 1780s by men who were advocates of a strong central government, such as Alexander Hamilton, John Marshall, and John Jay. With the pro-Federalist George Washington as the first president, the Federalists dominated the American political scene in the 1790s. Their opponents tended to align with Thomas Jefferson and his Republican or Democratic-Republican Party—which became the modern Democratic Party.

The Federalists tended to side with the wealthy: bankers, merchants, and other businessmen. As such, they became increasingly identified with a ruling class made up of those people, and not of the common people. Thus they were ill-prepared for the idea of democracy as the power of the people. As that idea grew in popularity, and such presidents as Thomas Jefferson advocated it, the Federalists fell further and further out of favor with the common American.

The Federalists favored stronger ties with Great Britain and a more powerful chief executive. However, they made a major miscalculation when they passed the unpopular Alien and Sedition Acts in 1798. After Washington's death in 1799, a split in the party between Hamilton and John Adams helped elect Jefferson as president in 1800. This split helped weaken the Federalist party further, hastening its demise.

The Federalists slowly lost influence during the terms of Jefferson and his successor, James Madison. The Federalists opposed the War of 1812, fought during the administration of James Madison, and they tried to capitalize on the war's unpopularity. However, by the end of the war, with Andrew Jackson's overwhelming victory against the British at New Orleans, Americans felt a wave of patriotism about the war. The Federalists were seen as the party of pessimism and defeat, and it hurt them.

By 1816, the Federalists were a viable political entity only in the northern American states. Ten years later, they had all but vanished from the political landscape.

*For Your Information*

A statue of Jefferson stands in the Thomas Jefferson Memorial. The memorial was dedicated in 1943, two hundred years after Jefferson's birth. Behind the statue are carved in stone the words he wrote as the preamble to the Declaration of Independence. Other passages from his writings are carved in other walls of the memorial.

# CHAPTER
# 5

## President Jefferson

The election left defeated President John Adams angry at Jefferson. He left Washington, D.C., at 4:00 A.M. on the day of Jefferson's inauguration so that he would not have to attend the event. Once close friends, Adams and Jefferson remained at odds for years.

Jefferson was inaugurated on March 4, 1801. Rejecting fancy balls and parties because they were not part of his values, after the ceremony the new President walked back to the boardinghouse in which he was staying and had dinner with the other lodgers.

Jefferson set out to remake the presidency according to what he believed were pure democratic principles. He decided not to present his State of the Union message as a speech before both houses of Congress, because he felt that resembled the way British kings opened sessions of Parliament. Instead, he sent a written message.

Jefferson brought new and different ideas to the presidency. He displayed natural history specimens in the White House. He also kept Dick, his pet mockingbird, in his office. Sometimes he opened Dick's cage and let him fly around the room.

Dressed in formal attire, the new British Minister to America was startled to have Jefferson receive him wearing casual clothes and old slippers. At formal dinners, Jefferson let everyone sit where they wanted, rather than use assigned seating according to rank.

While Jefferson tried to keep the United States out of European wars, he also was ready to defend American interests. This policy brought about one of his landmark achievements: the Louisiana Purchase.

Jefferson resurrected an idea that he had long favored: a scientific exploration of the western portion of America. At the time, Spain controlled New Orleans and the lower Mississippi River. Jefferson hoped that by making the United States a greater presence in the region, Spain would reconsider American colonization.

As he was planning the trip, Jefferson learned that France had taken over much of Spain's American territory. He sent Robert Livingston to France to try to buy New Orleans. At first the French turned him down. But then they made Livingston an amazing offer: They would sell not just New Orleans, but the entire Louisiana Territory, for $15 million—less than four cents per acre. The addition of the territory would double the size of the United States.

Delighted as he was by this sudden turn of events, Jefferson was worried. In his reading of the Constitution, he could find no place where it gave the federal government the power to spend money to buy land. He was so concerned about this point that he even drafted a constitutional amendment that allowed such purchases. Finally he decided that the purchase was too good to ignore. The United States and France signed treaties authorizing the sale on April 30, 1803. Lewis and Clark's subsequent exploration of the America interior to the Pacific Ocean proved invaluable to the American public.

Another important foreign policy issue that Jefferson faced was what to do about the Barbary Pirates. For years, ships of nations from the Barbary Coast of North Africa (Tunis, Algiers, Morocco, and Tripoli) ruled the Mediterranean Sea. They demanded money from nations whose ships used the area. If a country did not pay, their ships were often seized by the Barbary Pirates. The cargo was taken and the sailors imprisoned.

Once the U.S. became independent, its ships were no longer under the protection of Great Britain. American ships were routinely attacked and captured, and something had to be done.

In 1801, Jefferson sent a naval squadron to the Mediterranean to menace Tunis and Algiers, which broke their alliance with Tripoli. Fighting went on in that region for a few years, until another U.S.

raid in the area threatened to seize Tripoli and force its ruler from power. Ultimately a treaty between the U.S. and Tripoli was signed.

Domestically, Jefferson was unsuccessful at both trying to wipe out Hamilton's legacy and replacing Federalist judges whom Adams had appointed. But he enjoyed a domestic triumph of sorts when two of his greatest political enemies removed themselves from the scene. Vice President Aaron Burr and Alexander Hamilton fought a duel on July 11, 1804. Hamilton was killed, and Burr's political career was over.

Ironically, it was while Jefferson was trying to do something good that a scandal erupted whose echoes remain today. He pledged to repay any fines that Republican-leaning newspaper editors had incurred under the Alien and Sedition Acts. One of these editors was James Callendar, whom Jefferson had once used to attack Hamilton in print. Callendar wanted not only his fine repaid but a plum political office, which Jefferson did not want to give him—so Callendar turned against Jefferson. He accepted a job as editor of the *Richmond Recorder*, and began viciously attacking his former hero in print. His most sensational charge came on Septem-ber 1, 1802, when he accused Jefferson of having a relationship with one of his slaves—Sally Hemings. The relationship between Jefferson and Sally continues to be a source of controversy.

This charge did not stop Jefferson from winning a second term in 1804, with New York Governor George Clinton as his running mate. However, his second term was not as successful as his first. He was plagued by Republican politicians, who caused trouble for him over what they considered his misuse of executive power, such as in the Louisiana Purchase.

Jefferson also got into trouble over foreign affairs. He wanted desperately to keep America from becoming involved in European wars. As a result, he convinced Congress to pass the Embargo Act, which forbid American ships from trading with any European power. Jefferson had hoped to use the loss of American trade as a weapon to force warring European nations to make peace, but the idea backfired. The country whose economy was most devastated was America, particularly the New England area, and there was widespread anger at Jefferson as a result.

It was a weary Jefferson who wrote on March 2, 1809, just before his second presidential term ended: "Never did a prisoner released

The Louisiana Purchase doubled the size of the established United States. For $15 million, the United States received over 800,000 square miles of territory.

from his chains feel such relief as I shall on shaking off the shackles of power."[1]

When Jefferson left Washington for Monticello a few days later, after the inauguration of his successor James Madison, he finally had retired from politics for good. "Within a few days I shall bury myself in the groves of Monticello,"[2] he had said right before he left office, and he was as good as his word. Monticello became Jefferson's chief occupation. He worked on the house and grounds as long as he had the money to do so. Another project that took up much of his time was founding and designing the campus for the University of Virginia in nearby Charlottesville.

A happy by-product of Jefferson's retirement was the renewal of his friendship with John Adams. The two began trading letters in 1812, and kept in touch throughout the rest of their lives.

Jefferson had many visitors at Monticello. Some were prominent politically, such as Massachusetts Senator Daniel Webster and the Marquis de Lafayette, a Revolutionary War hero. Many others, however, were merely interested in the free food and drink at Monticello, for Jefferson was a perfect host and never turned anyone away. Unfortunately, these people often stayed far too long, draining the polite Jefferson's finances. Edmund Bacon, a worker at Monticello, recalled: "After Mr. Jefferson returned from Washington, he was for years crowded with visitors, and they almost ate him out of house and home. He knew that it more than used up all his income from the plantation and everything else; but he was so kind and polite that he received all his visitors with a smile, and made them welcome."[3]

Although he had earned a salary as president, Jefferson never made a lot of money in that position, nor from any other political office that he held. He felt that serving the public, and not making money, was its own reward. "When I first entered on the stage of public life (now twenty-four years ago)," he once said, "I came to a resolution never to engage, while in public office, in any kind of enterprise for improvement of my fortune, nor to wear, any other character than that of farmer."[4]

One way Jefferson got some money was by selling his library to Congress—nearly 6,500 books for about $24,000. However, the money he earned from the sale was quickly absorbed by his debts and expenses. In 1825, agricultural prices fell, putting Jefferson in enormous financial trouble. In order to save Monticello from creditors, friends raised money for him, and he sold much of his land.

All his life he had enjoyed good health, but in early 1826, as he approached his eighty-third birthday, he began to fail physically. He had diabetes, arthritis, a urinary tract infection, and perhaps even colon cancer. He was too frail to attend a special fiftieth anniversary celebration of the signing of the Declaration of Independence in Washington, D.C., that June. Jefferson treated the approach of death philosophically. "I am like an old watch, with a pinion worn out here, and a wheel there, until it can go no longer,"[5] he said.

On July 3 Jefferson got a fever. He managed to last until the afternoon of July 4, 1826. A few hours after his death, in Massachusetts, John Adams died, thinking that Jefferson was still alive. Two of the greatest men in American history thus passed away within hours of each other.

## The Lewis and Clark Expedition

The Lewis and Clark Expedition, which explored the vast territory that America bought from France in the Louisiana Purchase, is one of the great American achievements of all time.

Jefferson decided to outfit an expedition that would establish an American presence in the middle and western parts of the North American continent. He wanted the expedition to combine diplomatic, scientific, and commercial goals. To lead it he turned to his private secretary, Meriwether Lewis, an army officer and naturalist. Lewis tapped William Clark, brother of Revolutionary War hero George Rogers Clark, to help him.

The expedition set out from a camp outside St. Louis on May 21, 1804. Incredibly, despite the dangers of the mission, the only death the group suffered came shortly afterward, in August. A man named Charles Floyd died of what was apparently acute appendicitis.

The expedition had a scare when they first met the Lakota Sioux tribe of Native Americans. The Sioux wanted a boat as payment for letting the group cross their land. It appeared that a conflict between the two sides was imminent when, at the last moment, both sides took a step back and decided not to fight.

The explorers had another close call during the winter of 1804–1805 in present-day North Dakota. Trapped in their shelter without food, the men were saved when Shoshone Sacagawea and her husband brought them fish to eat.

Overall, the explorers covered about 8,000 miles—to the Pacific Ocean and back. Although it didn't discover a Northwest Passage—a water route connecting the Atlantic and Pacific oceans that was popularly believed to exist—the expedition made peaceful contact with numerous Native American peoples, and catalogued a vast amount of information about the geography, plants, and animals of the western United States.

Meriwether Lewis died in 1809 of a mysterious gunshot wound. Whether he was murdered or committed suicide is a mystery, although reportedly he was extremely depressed right before he died. Thus it fell to William Clark to finish the group's report.

# Chapter Notes

## Chapter 2  Gentleman Farmer

1. E. M. Halliday, *Understanding Thomas Jefferson* (New York: HarperCollins Publishers, 2001), p. 29.
2. Carl Binger, *Thomas Jefferson—A Well-Tempered Mind* (New York: W.W. Norton & Company, Inc., 1970), p. 62.

## Chapter 3  Revolution at Home and Abroad

1. R. B. Bernstein, *Thomas Jefferson* (New York: Oxford University Press, 2003), p. 32.
2. Ibid.
3. Ibid, p. 47.
4. *Thomas Jefferson—A Biography in His Own Words*, by the editors of Newsweek Books (New York: Newsweek, 1974), p. 79.
5. Ibid., p. 80.
6. Carl Binger, *Thomas Jefferson—A Well-Tempered Mind* (New York: W.W. Norton & Company, Inc., 1970), p. 97.
7. E. M. Halliday, *Understanding Thomas Jefferson* (New York: HarperCollins Publishers, 2001), p. 9.

## Chapter 4 Hamilton and Home

1. Carl Binger, *Thomas Jefferson—A Well-Tempered Mind* (New York, W.W. Norton & Company, Inc., 1970), p. 148.
2. R. B. Bernstein, *Thomas Jefferson* (New York: Oxford University Press, 2003), p. 99.
3. Ibid.
4. Ibid., p. 100.
5. Ibid., p. 103.
6. Ibid., p. 105.

## Chapter 5  President Jefferson

1. R. B. Bernstein, *Thomas Jefferson* (New York: Oxford University Press, 2003), p. 169.
2. Fawn M. Brodie, *Thomas Jefferson—An Intimate History* (New York: Bantam Books, Inc. 1974), p. 574.
3. Bernstein, p. 182.
4. Carl Binger, *Thomas Jefferson—A Well-Tempered Mind* (New York, W.W. Norton & Company, Inc., 1970), p. 18.
5. Ibid., p. 19.

# Chronology

| | |
|---|---|
| 1743 | Born in April in Shadwell, Virginia |
| 1757 | Father, Peter Jefferson, dies |
| 1760–62 | Attends the College of William and Mary |
| 1767 | Is admitted to practice law |
| 1768 | Is elected to Virginia House of Burgesses |
| 1770 | Construction begins at Monticello; he moves into unfinished house |
| 1772 | Marries Martha Wayles Skelton; daughter Martha is born |
| 1774 | Writes *A Summary View of the Rights of British America*; retires from law; daughter Jane Randolph is born |
| 1775 | Is elected to Continental Congress; daughter Jane Randolph dies |
| 1776 | Writes Declaration of Independence; is asked to revise Virginia laws; mother dies |
| 1777 | Writes *Virginia Statute for Religious Freedom*; unnamed son is born and dies |
| 1778 | British reach Monticello to arrest Jefferson and legislators, who escape to Staunton; daughter Mary (Maria) is born |
| 1779–1781 | Serves as governor of Virginia |
| 1780 | Daughter Lucy Elizabeth is born |
| 1781 | Daughter Lucy Elizabeth dies |
| 1782 | Second daughter named Lucy Elizabeth is born; wife, Martha, dies on September 6 |
| 1783 | Is delegate to Congress |
| 1784–1789 | Is ambassador to France |
| 1784 | Second Lucy Elizabeth dies |
| 1786 | General Assembly passes his *Virginia Statute for Religious Freedom* |
| 1790–1793 | Serves as first secretary of state |
| 1797–1801 | Serves as vice president of the United States |
| 1797–1815 | Serves as president of the American Philosophical Society |
| 1801–1809 | Serves as third U.S. president |
| 1803 | Asks Livingston to negotiate the Louisiana Purchase; arranges Lewis and Clark expedition |
| 1804 | Daughter Maria dies |
| 1806 | Builds house at Poplar Forest |
| 1809 | Retires from public life |
| 1815 | Sells library to U.S. Congress |
| 1825 | The University of Virginia opens |
| 1826 | Dies on July 4, fifty years after the Declaration of Independence is signed |

# Timeline in History

| | |
|---|---|
| **1700** | America's colonial population is about 275,000 people. |
| **1704** | Deerfield, Massachusetts, is destroyed as a result of Queen Anne's War. |
| **1705** | Laws restricting slave travel are passed by New York, Virginia, and Massachusetts. |
| **1713** | The South Sea Company of England is allowed to bring nearly 5,000 slaves per year into Spanish North America. |
| **1718** | New Orleans and San Antonio are founded. |
| **1720** | America's colonial population is about 474,000 people. |
| **1724** | Jewish settlers are outlawed from Louisiana. |
| **1749** | Georgia, a colony that had banned slavery, makes it legal. |
| **1754–1763** | French and Indian War between England and France is fought. |
| **1765** | The British Parliament passes the Stamp Act. |
| **1766–1767** | Daniel Boone journeys to Kentucky. |
| **1773** | Patriots protest taxation without representation by staging the Boston Tea Party. |
| **1775** | Fighting at Lexington and Concord begins the American Revolution. |
| **1776** | Declaration of Independence is adopted. Mission of San Francisco de Asis is founded. |
| **1781** | British surrender at Yorktown, Virginia. |
| **1787** | The Constitutional Convention meets in Philadelphia to draft a successor to the Articles of Confederation. |
| **1789** | George Washington becomes the first United States president. |
| **1794** | The federal government uses military force against citizens in the Whiskey Rebellion. |
| **1796** | John Adams becomes president. Tennessee becomes a slaveholding state. |
| **1800** | John "Johnny Appleseed" Chapman begins giving out apple seeds and seedlings in Ohio. |
| **1804** | Alexander Hamilton is killed in a duel with Aaron Burr. |
| **1808** | The Native American Osage tribe loses land in Missouri and Arkansas to the United States. |
| **1810** | John Jacob Astor founds the Pacific Fur Company. |
| **1812** | Louisiana enters the Union. War of 1812 begins. |
| **1816** | Indiana is admitted to the Union. |
| **1820** | Missouri Compromise is passed in an effort to seek a balance between slave and free states. Frontiersman Daniel Boone dies. |
| **1825** | Erie Canal, which connects the Great Lakes to the Hudson River, is completed. |
| **1826** | Both Thomas Jefferson and John Adams die on the same day. |
| **1831** | First issue of *The Liberator*, an antislavery newspaper, is published. |
| **1836** | Texas freedom fighters die at the Battle of the Alamo. |
| **1838** | The Underground Railroad is organized to help people flee slavery. |
| **1841** | William Henry Harrison becomes first U.S. president to die in office. |
| **1845** | Texas becomes the twenty-eighth American state. |
| **1848** | Gold is discovered in California. |
| **1861** | The Civil War begins. |

# Further Reading

**For Young Adults**

Barrett, Marvin. *Meet Thomas Jefferson*. New York: Random House, 2001.

Bober, Natalie. *Thomas Jefferson: Man on a Mountain*. New York: Aladdin, 1997.

Ferris, Jeri Chase. *Thomas Jefferson: Father of Liberty*. Minneapolis: Carolrhoda Books, 1998.

Hargrove, Jim. *Thomas Jefferson: Third President of the United States*. Chicago: Childrens Press, 1986.

Old, Wendie C. *Thomas Jefferson*. Springfield, N.J.: Enslow Publishers, 1997.

Severance, John B. *Thomas Jefferson: Architect of Democracy*. New York: Clarion Books, 1998.

**Works Consulted**

Bernstein, R. B. *Thomas Jefferson*. New York: Oxford University Press, 2003.

Binger, Carl. *Thomas Jefferson—A Well-Tempered Mind*. New York: W.W. Norton & Company, Inc., 1970.

Brodie, Fawn M. *Thomas Jefferson—An Intimate History*. New York: Bantam Books, Inc. 1974.

Halliday, E. M. *Understanding Thomas Jefferson*. New York: HarperCollins Publishers, 2001.

Malone, Dumas. *The Sage of Monticello*. Boston: Little, Brown, 1981.

*Thomas Jefferson—A Biography in His Own Words*, by the editors of Newsweek Books. New York: Newsweek, 1974.

**On the Internet**

Monticello: The Home of Thomas Jefferson
**http://www.monticello.org**

The Library of Congress: The Thomas Jefferson Papers
**http://memory.loc.gov/ammem/collections/jefferson_papers/**

University of Virginia: The Thomas Jefferson Digital Archive
**http://etext.virginia.edu/jefferson/**

The Works of Thomas Jefferson
**http://libertyonline.hypermall.com/Jefferson/index.html**

American Presidents: Thomas Jefferson
**http://www.americanpresidents.org/presidents/president.asp?PresidentNumber=3**

Thomas Jefferson—Sally Hemings DNA Study
**http://www.angelfire.com/va/TJTruth/**

Poplar Forest—Retreat Home of Thomas Jefferson
**http://www.poplarforest.org**

# Glossary

**abstain (ab-STAYN)**
To voluntarily stop from doing something.

**accumulate (ah-KYOO-myoo-layt)**
To add up, collect, or gather.

**appall (uh-PAWL)**
To fill with horror or dismay.

**appendicitis (uh-pen-dih-SYE-tis)**
An inflammation of the appendix, an organ found in the human body.

**cabinet (KAA-bih-net)**
A group of advisers to the president.

**concessions (kon-SEH-shuns)**
Surrendering or compromise.

**defer (duh-FUR)**
To step down; to put off until sometime in the future.

**deport (de-PORT)**
To expel from a country.

**dumbwaiter (DUM-way-tur)**
A small elevator-like device used to move food between floors.

**harpsichord (HARP-sih-kord)**
A keyboard instrument that was used before the piano.

**orator (OR-uh-ter)**
A persuasive speaker.

**pinion (PIN-yin)**
A small gear wheel that is designed to mesh with a larger gear wheel or rack.

**skeptic (SKEP-tik)**
Someone who has doubts about a belief.

**tenure (TEN-yur)**
The period or term of holding on to a position or office.

**viable (VYE-uh-bul)**
Capable of growing and developing.

# Index

Adams, Abigail    23, 24
Adams, John    16, 20, 22, 23, 24, 32,
    33, 34, 35, 37, 39, 40, 41
Alien and Sedition Acts    34, 35, 39
American Philosophical Society    32
Arnold, Benedict    21
Burr, Aaron    32, 33 34, 39
Callendar, James    25, 39
Clinton, George    39
College of William and Mary    10,
    12
Continental Congress    17
Cosway, Marie    24
Federalist Party    17, 30, 35
Franklin, Benjamin    16, 20, 22, 23,
    26, 32
George III    6, 15, 19
Genet Affair    30–31
Hamilton, Alexander    26, 27–30,
    32, 34, 35, 39
Hemings, Betty    14
Hemings, Madison    25
Hemings, Sally    14, 25, 39
Henry, Patrick    7, 12, 13, 14, 17
Jackson, Andrew    35
Jay, John    22, 35
Jefferson, Jane (sister)    11
Jefferson, Jane Randolph (mother)
    11
Jefferson, Lucy (daughter)    21, 22,
    23
Jefferson, Peter (father)    11, 12
Jefferson, Martha (daughter)    7, 22,
    23, 27, 31
Jefferson, Martha (wife)    7, 9, 12,
    13, 14, 18, 21–22
Jefferson, Mary (daughter)    7, 22
Jefferson, Thomas
    as architect    9
    birth of    11
    death of    41
    education of    12
    as governor of Virginia    7–8,
        20–21
    as inventor    31
    as lawyer    12
    marriage of    12–13
    in Paris    23–34
    as president of the United States
        34, 37–40
    as secretary of state    27–31
    and slavery    14, 23, 25, 31–32
    as vice president    32–34
    in Virginia House of Burgesses
        12, 14
    writes Declaration of
        Independence    16, 19–20,
        22, 36
Jefferson Memorial    36
Jouett, Jack    7
Knox, Henry    27
L'Enfant, Pierre Charles    28
Livingston, Robert    16, 38
Louisiana Purchase    38, 39, 40
Madison, James    31, 35, 40
*Manual of Parliamentary Practice,
    A*    32–33
Monroe, James    10, 21, 31
Monticello    7–8, 9, 12–15, 22, 25,
    31, 32, 40–41
*Notes on the State of Virginia*    24
Pinckney, Charles    34
Pinckney, Thomas    32, 33
Poplar Forest    9
Randolph, Edmund    27
Randolph, Thomas Jefferson    31
Randolph, Thomas Mann    27
Sherman, Roger    16
*Summary View of the Rights of
    British America, A*    6, 14
University of Virginia    40
Washington, George    10, 14, 16, 20,
    27, 28, 30, 31, 32, 35
Washington, D.C.    28, 29, 40
Wayles, John    14
Wirt, William    17
Wythe, George    12
XYZ Affair    33–34

48